Protecting Our Planet

What Can We Do About TOXINS IN THE ENVIRONMENT?

David J. Jakubiak

PowerKiDS press.

New York

For librarians like Nancy Colby, who introduce children to the wonder of books

Published in 2012 by The Rosen Publishing Group, Inc.
29 East 21st Street, New York, NY 10010

First Edition

Editor: Amelie von Zumbusch
Book Design: Kate Laczynski
Layout Design: Julio Gil

Photo Credits: Cover Bo Tornvig/Getty Images; pp. 4 (main), 8, 10, 16, 20 Shutterstock.com; p. 4 (inset) Scott Olson/Getty Images; p. 6 Nacivet/Getty Images; p. 12 Sankei via Getty Images; p. 14 Luis Acosta/AFP/Getty Images; p. 16 © www.iStockphoto.com/blackwaterimages; p. 18 iStockphoto/Thinkstock.

Library of Congress Cataloging-in-Publication Data

Jakubiak, David J.
 What can we do about toxins in the environment? / by David J. Jakubiak. — 1st ed.
    p. cm. — (Protecting our planet)
 Includes index.
 ISBN 978-1-4488-4987-1 (library binding) — ISBN 978-1-4488-5121-8 (pbk.) — ISBN 978-1-4488-5122-5 (6-pack)
 1. Environmental toxicology—Juvenile literature. 2. Toxins—Juvenile literature. I. Title. II. Series.
 RA1226.J35 2012
 615.9′02—dc22

                                    2011000151

Manufactured in the United States of America

CPSIA Compliance Information: Batch #WS11PK: For Further Information contact Rosen Publishing, New York, New York at 1-800-237-9932

CONTENTS

WARNING

UNSAFE WATERS

YOU SHOULD NOT SWIM
IN THESE WATERS

YOU SHOULD NOT EAT FISH
FROM THESE WATERS

The Indiana Department of Environmental Management
is currently working on a Remedial Action Plan (RAP)
to restore these waters.
For more information, contact IDEM at (2l7)881-6712

People like to fish in Lake Michigan. Inset: Some rivers that flow into Lake Michigan are unsafe for fishing. Toxic substances were dumped there.

4

It's Toxic!

Killer whales are some of the most powerful animals in the sea. However, something tiny is hurting some of them. Scientists have found that the animals have lots of **polychlorinated biphenyls**, or PCBs, in their bodies. PCBs are **chemicals** that used to be in things like paint and electrical wires. The PCBs in killer whales' bodies are making them sick.

PCBs are toxic. This means that they hurt living things. Today, there are toxic **substances**, or things, in our air, dirt, food, and water. They can hurt both people and animals. All of us have some PCBs and other toxic substances in our bodies. Having too much of a toxic substance will make us sick.

This man is spraying pesticides on apple trees. This will keep bugs from eating the apples. Most pesticides are toxic, though.

Many toxic substances in the **environment**, or world around us, got there because of people. Some things people do to make our lives easier make toxic chemicals. Power plants make the electricity to light our homes and schools. They also release some toxic chemicals into the air. Factories may release toxic substances when they make things such as frying pans.

People also use toxic chemicals to do certain jobs. For example, toxic chemicals called **pesticides** kill bugs that eat crops and spread sickness. Chemicals that make goods better can be toxic, too. Some chemicals that are used to make plastics stronger or softer are toxic.

DID YOU KNOW?

Toxic chemicals can get into food from plastic containers. When plastic is heated or gets old, the chemicals may leak into food.

Cell phones are very handy. However, the phones have toxic substances in them that can leak out after they have been thrown away.

Sticking Around

Toxic substances can get into the air, water, and soil in many ways. Factories used to dump PCBs into rivers. Every time that someone who is using medicine flushes the toilet, chemicals go down the drain. They can end up in rivers, lakes, and oceans. Pesticides on crops get washed away by the rain. Toxic substances also leak out of garbage dumps.

Once toxic substances are in the environment, it is hard to get rid of them. The United States stopped using PCBs in the 1970s. However, they are still found in the environment. Some scientists worry that the PCBs in certain killer whales may not go away until 2063.

DID YOU KNOW?

Medicines that leaked into some lakes and rivers are causing some male fish there to turn into females. These medicines are toxic to the fish.

This otter and the fish it is eating are both part of a food chain. Hunters, like this otter, are at the top of food chains.

Moving Up the Food Chain

Plants and tiny living things called **plankton** take in toxic chemicals from the water or air. Small animals, such as tiny fish, eat plants and plankton. They take in the chemicals, too. Larger animals, such as salmon and seals, eat lots of these smaller animals. The living things that depend on each other for food make up a **food chain**. Once toxic chemicals enter a food chain, they spread quickly. Animals at the top of a food chain, such as killer whales, have the most toxins in their bodies.

People are part of the food chain, too. When we eat things that have toxic chemicals in them, the chemicals build up in our bodies. Sometimes, these chemicals make us sick.

Red tide gets its name because it turns the water red. This outbreak of red tide happened in the waters off of Kobe, Japan.

Naturally Toxic

People are to blame for many of the toxic substances in the environment. However, others are made naturally. In 2004, 107 bottlenose dolphins died off the coast of Florida. Scientists collected some of the bodies and did tests to find out why. They found that toxins made by **algae** had poisoned the dolphins. Algae are tiny things that live in water.

Sometimes algae grow out of control. These huge amounts of algae make the water look red. This is called a red tide. Red tides can poison fish and shellfish. Animals or people who eat those fish and shellfish can get sick and die.

DID YOU KNOW?

Mold can also make toxins. Fuzzy patches of mold are made up of thousands of tiny living things. Too much mold can make people sick.

This toy is being tested for lead. It was found to have lead in it. It and thousands of other toys with lead in them then had to be destroyed.

Dangerous Toys

Have you ever had to return a toy because your parents said it was unsafe? Many children have because they had toys with **lead** in them. Lead is one of several toxic metals. **Mercury** is another metal that is toxic.

People have known for a long time that lead can be harmful to children. Children who have too much lead in their bodies may have problems learning. The United States has tried to keep children safe by banning lead in gasoline and paint. However, some old houses still have lead paint on their walls. Some countries still use lead paint on toys and other goods, too.

DID YOU KNOW?

Loons living in some New York lakes are in danger. The fish they eat have mercury in them, which makes the loons sick. The mercury came from burning coal.

Frogs have thin skin that lets in outside substances. This is one reason that toxic substances cause so many problems for frogs.

Fears for Frogs

Something terrible is happening to frogs. Many frogs have been found with too many legs or too few. Frogs are getting **infections** that make them sick and hurt their brains. Some male frogs are starting to look and act more like female frogs. Scientists found out that certain pesticides are to blame for these problems.

Pesticides are used to kill bugs, mold, and other things that can destroy food crops such as corn. When the pesticides are sprayed on crops, though, the rain washes them into nearby ponds where frogs live. In ponds where there are a lot of pesticides, frogs do not grow properly. They get sick more easily, too.

The bald eagle is the national bird of the United States. Since 2007, it is no longer listed as endangered, or in danger of dying out, there.

One kind of toxic pesticide almost wiped out bald eagles in the United States. However, efforts to save the birds have helped them make a comeback.

The pesticide was DDT. It was used to kill mosquitoes. It would wash into lakes and get into fish. When eagles ate the fish, it made the shells of their eggs soft. The eggs would break when the parents sat on them to keep them warm. To help eagles and other birds, the U.S. government banned DDT in 1972. Since that time, the numbers of bald eagles living in the United States has grown. Today, bald eagles are doing well.

DID YOU KNOW?

Bald eagles are not the only birds that were hurt by DDT. It also made brown pelican and peregrine falcon eggs easily breakable.

This farmer raises plants without the use of toxic pesticides. The food he grows is safer for eaters and for the environment in general.

Cleaning Up

Since toxic substances stay in the environment for so long, the best way to keep people and animals safe is to stop them from ever getting there. Today, many factories and power plants put **scrubbers** on their smokestacks. The scrubbers keep mercury and other toxic substances from getting out. People recycle batteries and lightbulbs that have toxic metals in them.

Some farmers have stopped using pesticides. They use insects, such as ladybugs and praying mantises, to eat bugs. Companies are making paints and other products that do not have lead or toxic chemicals in them. At home, some families are using vinegar and water to clean instead of toxic cleaners.

Making Safe Choices

Kids need to stay away from toxic substances. Their brains and bodies are still growing. Toxic substances can change the way these things happen. There are plenty of things that kids can do to keep themselves safe, though. Remember to wash your hands after being outside. Never put jewelry or toys in your mouth. Do not touch bug spray or toxic cleaners. Leave that to adults.

It is also important to watch what you eat. Always wash fruits and vegetables before you eat them. Avoid eating fish that have lots of toxic substances, such as mercury, in them. Work with your parents to find out which fish are safe to eat. With a little effort, you can keep yourself safe!

GLOSSARY

algae (AL-jee) Plantlike living things without roots or stems that live in water.

chemicals (KEH-mih-kulz) Matter that can be mixed with other matter to cause changes.

environment (en-VY-ern-ment) Everything that surrounds people and other living things and everything that makes it possible for them to live.

food chain (FOOD CHAYN) A group of living things that are each other's food.

infections (in-FEK-shunz) Sicknesses caused by germs.

lead (LED) A heavy metal that can make people sick if it gets in their bodies.

mercury (MER-kyuh-ree) A poisonous, silver-colored element.

pesticides (PES-tuh-sydz) Poisons used to kill pests.

plankton (PLANK-ten) Plants and animals that drift with water currents.

polychlorinated biphenyls (po-lee-KLAWR-uh-nay-ted by-FEH-nulz) A group of chemicals. They hurt living things.

scrubbers (SKRUH-berz) Things put on smokestacks to clean the smoke.

substances (SUB-stan-siz) Any matter that takes up space.

INDEX

A
algae, 13
animals, 5, 11, 13, 21

B
bodies, 5, 11, 13, 15, 22

C
chemicals, 5, 7, 9, 11, 21

D
dirt, 5

F
food, 5, 11

I
infections, 17

K
killer whales, 5, 9, 11

L
lead, 15, 21

M
mercury, 15, 21–22

P
paint(s), 5, 15, 21
pesticide(s), 7, 9, 17, 19, 21

polychlorinated biphenyls (PCBs), 5, 9

S
scientists, 5, 9, 13, 17
scrubbers, 21
sea, 5

T
toxic substances, 5, 7, 9, 13, 21–22

W
water, 5, 9, 11, 13, 21
wires, 5

WEB SITES

Due to the changing nature of Internet links, PowerKids Press has developed an online list of Web sites related to the subject of this book. This site is updated regularly. Please use this link to access the list:

www.powerkidslinks.com/pop/toxins/